The Story of

OLYMPIC DIVER

SAMMY LEE

The Story of
OLYMPIC DIVER
SAMMY LEE

by **Paula Yoo**
additional material by **Cheryl Kim**
with illustrations by **Dom Lee**

WITHDRAWN

Lee & Low Books Inc.
New York

I would like to acknowledge and thank Dr. Sammy Lee for his generous time and inspirational life story. Special thanks also to my editor, Phillip Lee; Steven Malk of Writers House; Dom and Keunhee Lee; Anne Park; Sandy Tanaka; Janie Bynum; Carolyn Crimi; Kelly DiPucchio; April Young Fritz; Hope Vestergaard; and Lisa Wheeler—P.Y.

Photo credits: p.14: Helen Panayi/Swim England • p.16: public domain The Public Domain Review • p.27: Courtesy of the Center for Korean Studies, University of Hawai'i at Mānoa • p.29: public domain National Archives Catalogue identifier 520796 • p.38: Courtesy of the Everett Collection • p.40: public domain/courtesy of Densho Digital Repository • p.52: Marcello Farina / Shutterstock.com • p.57: AP/Wide World Photos • p.60: AP Photo/Michael Conroy

LEE & LOW BOOKS Inc. , 95 Madison Avenue, New York, NY 10016
leeandlow.com
Edited by Phillip Lee and Kandace Coston
Book design by NeuStudio
Book production by The Kids at Our House
Manufactured in the United States of America by Lake Book Manufacturing, Inc.

The text is set in Vollkorn
The display font is set in Avenir Next
The illustrations are rendered in oil wash with kneaded erasures.
10 9 8 7 6 5 4 3 2 1
First Edition
Cataloging-in-Publication Data on file with the Library of Congress
ISBN 978-1-64379-014-5

*For my family: Young and Kim Yoo, David Yoo,
and Kyle McCorkle—P.Y.*

*To the first generation of Koreans who accomplished
the American Dream—D.L.*

TABLE OF CONTENTS

CHAPTER ONE

SAMMY'S SOMERSAULT

The sign at the swimming pool read MEMBERS ONLY.

Twelve-year-old Sammy Lee knew exactly what that sign meant—only whites were permitted to enter even though it was a public pool. This was the practice in 1932. Sammy would have to wait until Wednesday when people of color were allowed to go inside. In the meantime, he would get no relief from the blazing California summer sun.

Sammy clutched the chain-link gate. He gazed in **envy** at the children splashing and shouting in the water. He watched as a boy stood on the diving board and held out his arms. The boy flew high in the air and broke the surface of the water with hardly a splash.

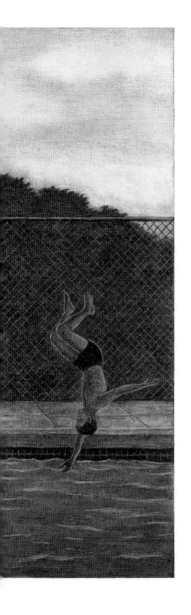

I want to learn how to do that, Sammy thought.

The following Wednesday, Sammy was the first one through the open gate. He raced to the springboard, stood on the edge, and spread his arms like wings. He took a deep breath and leaped as high as he could.

Sammy soared. *I'm flying*, he thought. He tucked his knees against his chest and spun into a **somersault**.

SPLAT!

Sammy splashed everyone, including his friend Hart Crum, who was also limited to using the pool on Wednesdays because he was African American.

Hart challenged Sammy to do more than one somersault. Sammy, eager to show off, raced back to the springboard. Try as he might, Sammy could only complete one somersault.

Hart stopped teasing Sammy and offered to help him instead. He followed Sammy onto the diving board and together they jumped. When they landed, Hart's extra weight helped Sammy leap higher into the air. This time Sammy completed one and a half somersaults before hitting the water! He grinned, eager to practice again with Hart.

Sammy Lee was born on August 1, 1920, in Fresno, California, the youngest child of SoonKee and EunKee Chun Rhee. They later moved to Highland Park, California, where Sammy grew up with his two older sisters, Dolly and Mary. Over the summer, Sammy discovered he had a natural talent for diving, but his father wanted him to stop wasting time with sports and instead become a doctor. Sammy's parents had left Korea for a better life in America. His father worked hard at their family's restaurant, saving money in the bank and putting his tips in a shoebox for his son's future. "In America," Sammy's father said, "you can achieve anything if you set your heart to it."

One morning Sammy and his father drove to the market downtown to pick up vegetables for their restaurant. The streets were lined with flags from different countries. Sammy's father explained that Los Angeles was hosting the Olympics and the flags represented the participating countries. The gold medal winners were considered the greatest athletes in the world.

A chill ran through Sammy. Although his father wanted him to be a doctor, Sammy knew he wanted to be an Olympic champion.

Diving into Diving

Modern competitive diving involves jumping from a diving board and performing **acrobatic** stunts in the air while plunging toward a body of water. There are two different types of diving boards. A *springboard* is a flexible, bouncy board positioned one to three meters (3.3 to 9.8 feet) above the surface of the water. A springboard's flexibility allows divers to jump high

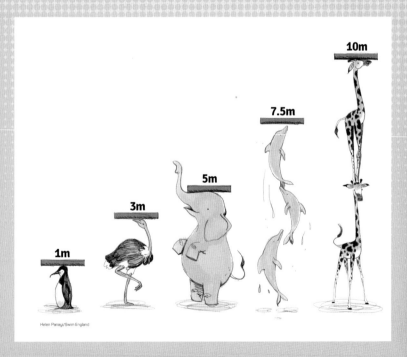

Helen Panayi/Swim England

Diagram of different heights of diving boards compared to the heights of animals.

in the air, giving them more time to **execute** various moves before entering the water. A *platform board* is a firm board positioned at 5, 7.5, or 10 meters above the water. (Ten meters equals 33 feet—the height of two female giraffes!)

Jumping from a higher height allows a diver to complete more acrobatics during their fall, but it is also more dangerous: a diver can enter the water at speeds up to 40 miles per hour (mph). The techniques required to dive from a springboard are different from those used on a platform board. Many of the world's best divers focus on diving from one board or the other.

There are six main types of dives. A dive is named by the direction the diver is facing before taking off from the diving board and the direction the diver will rotate after taking off from the board:

- Forward (forward takeoff with forward rotation)
- Backward (backward takeoff with backward rotation)
- Reverse (forward takeoff with backward rotation)
- Inward (backward takeoff with forward rotation)
- Twister (any of the above dives that also uses a

forward, backward, reverse, or inward twist)

- Arm Stand (a platform dive that begins in a hand-stand position)

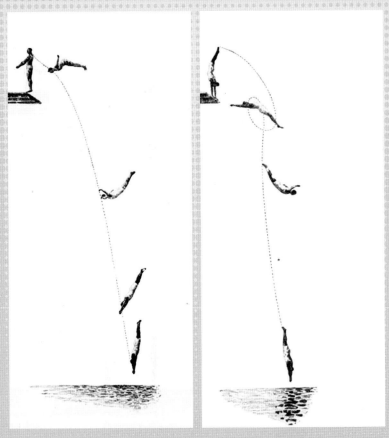

Two illustrations of a diver performing a backwards dive with inward rotation (left) and an arm stand dive with a somersault.

In addition to the forward or backward takeoff and rotation, a diver's body can be in one of the following positions:

- Straight: the diver's body is fully extended
- Pike: the diver's body is only bent at the hips
- Tuck: the diver's body is bent at the hips and knees
- Free: a combination of the three positions above, used only in twisting dives.

For swimmers who want to get involved with the sport of diving, the first step is to contact a local diving club. Some clubs offer programs where kids can learn diving with a coach who teaches the safety skills and basics necessary for beginner and advanced diving. Diving as a sport is not only about learning fun techniques, but also an opportunity for athletes to develop self-confidence and self-discipline, face challenges, overcome fears, and become team players.

CHAPTER TWO
SCHOOL AND SPORTS

Sammy decided that diving would be his ticket to the Olympics, but he knew that sooner or later he would have to find a coach to help him improve his diving skills. He couldn't just rely on his friend Hart giving him advice.

In the summer of 1938, when he was eighteen, Sammy

attended a swim and diving competition. Between meets he sneaked into the pool area to practice. When Sammy came up for air after his first dive, he heard one of the coaches shout, "That's the **lousiest** dive I've ever seen!"

Sammy spotted a tall, heavyset man at the edge of the pool. "You get back up there and practice until I say you can quit," the man barked. "Stand straight! Spread your arms out more! Your **arch** is too deep!" Sammy wondered why this stranger was suddenly giving him orders. He obeyed anyway, curious to see if the man's advice would help improve his dives. By the end of the day, Sammy was exhausted, but he had never dived better.

"I'm Jim Ryan," the man finally said. "I'm your new coach."

Because Sammy could only use the local pool one day a week, Coach Ryan had him dig a giant hole in the coach's backyard. They filled this pit with sand and installed a diving board above it.

Sammy trained every day in that sandpit. The gritty sand filled his ears, and his palms were lined with grime. When it rained, the wet sand weighed down his swimming trunks. Once, Sammy slipped and cut his forehead, but he didn't give up. He never disobeyed Coach Ryan's endless orders.

To keep from hurting himself, Sammy had to land on his feet after each dive into the sandpit. So he enrolled in a gymnastics class at school to help develop stronger leg muscles. As a result, Sammy was able to jump much higher off the diving board than other divers. Performing difficult dives became easy for him, and Sammy earned a **reputation** for his graceful and seemingly effortless dives.

Although Sammy was exhausted every night from a full day of school followed by diving practice and homework, he managed to keep up his grades and earn all A's. Sammy's classmates voted him Most Likely to Succeed, and he was the first nonwhite student elected as student body president. Occidental College in Los Angeles, impressed with Sammy's achievements, offered him a full scholarship.

Despite his academic and athletic success, Sammy still faced **discrimination**. During his senior year of high school, Sammy could not attend his own prom. The party was held at the Pasadena Civic Auditorium, and only white students were allowed to enter.

That injustice angered Sammy. How could his father insist Sammy could achieve anything in America when he wasn't even allowed to attend his own prom?

Diving was the only world where Sammy felt he belonged. Even though he had graduated at the top of his high school class, his grades dropped during his first year of college because he spent more time diving than studying.

Sammy and his father fought over his grades. Sammy didn't understand why his father refused to support his dream of becoming an Olympic champion.

Then one afternoon Sammy witnessed a rude customer **berating** his father at the restaurant.

Later, Sammy asked his father how he could allow people to treat him that way. His father answered that instead of losing his temper, he acted with honor. He explained that if Sammy became a doctor, he would get the respect he deserved. "In America, you can achieve anything if you set your heart to it," he reminded Sammy.

For the first time, Sammy understood why his father pressured him to do well in school. So he struck a deal with his father. Sammy could dive as long as his grades were good enough for medical school.

How Koreans Came to the United States

In 1882 the US government passed the **Chinese Exclusion Act**, which prohibited Chinese workers from immigrating to the US. This **legislation** also banned US plantation owners from recruiting cheap laborers from China, so the owners turned to Korea for a new source of labor. Around the same time, during the early 1900s, Japan invaded Korea which forced many Korean families to abandon their homes as Japanese soldiers took control of the country. Many walked for several days until they reached a port in Inchon City, where American **recruiters** waited with ships ready to take Korean laborers to work on sugar and pineapple plantations in Hawaii.

Desperate to leave their country in the midst of drought, famine, and political **instability,** many Korean men signed a labor contract, which promised wages and free passage to Hawaii in exchange for three to five years of work. Within two years, more than 7,000

Koreans arrived in Hawaii in hopes of finding a higher quality of living for themselves and their families.

When their labor contracts ended, about half of the Korean immigrants returned to Korea, while the other half moved to the mainland United States. Many worked as gardeners, janitors, and domestic servants while others set up small businesses such as laundromats, nail salons, restaurants, and grocery stores.

Since most of the original immigrants were men, more than two thousand "picture brides" came from Korea to Hawaii and California between 1905 and 1924 to marry **bachelor** immigrants. Most of these young women were between 18 and 24 years old and from poor, rural areas. A matchmaker would pair the picture bride with a Korean husband living in the US using only their photographs. Some photographs of potential husbands were from previous decades or staged in front of a large plantation to portray a younger and wealthier version of the man being matched. Many picture brides who looked forward to marrying a young and wealthy man were disappointed when they arrived in the US and met their husband in person. The large number of Korean women entering America brought about a new generation of American-born Koreans, who would grow up to have more opportunities than their parents. This first wave of Korean immigrants ended when Congress passed the **Immigration Act of 1924,** which limited the number of immigrants entering the United States.

Photo of a twenty-one-year-old Korean picture bride, circa 1920.

The second wave of immigrants to the US started during the **Korean War** (1950–1953). From 1910 to 1945, Japan invaded and occupied Korea. After Japan was defeated in **World War II** (1939–1945), Korea split into two separate countries. In June 1950, North Korea invaded South Korea, sparking the Korean War. Due to South Korea's strong military, political, and economic ties with the United States, approximately 15,000 Korean men, women, and children immigrated to the US between 1950 and 1964 to escape the conflict. The **War Bride Act** also allowed American servicemen in Korea to bring their Korean wives and children to the United States, which also contributed to the number of immigrants entering the US. Finally, the **Immigration and Nationality Act of 1952** put an end to the Oriental Exclusion Act by allowing a specific number of Koreans to immigrate to America and giving them the opportunity to become US citizens. This included Korean War orphans adopted by American families and around 27,000 businessmen, professionals, and students.

A Korean girl carrying her brother past a stalled M-26 tank, in Haengju, Korea, during the Korean War, 1951.

The third wave of Korean immigrants arrived in the US after Congress passed the **Immigration and Nationality Act of 1965.** This act removed the limitations on the number of people immigrating to the US that were established in the Immigration and Nationality Act of 1952. With this new legislation, the United States government gave preference to immigrants with US relatives, refugees of violence, and professionals with "useful skills" such as doctors, scientists, engineers, and mathematicians.

From 1960 to 1975, South Korea experienced a major period of industrialization and population growth, from 25 million to 35 million people. This increase in the number of available workers led to a decrease in the **minimum wage** because companies knew they could pay workers less money since workers had few job options. To address the lack of job opportunities for the rising number of people, the South Korean government encouraged **emigration** to help control the country's population. Many middle-class Korean families decided to leave South Korea to find work and make more money. Between 1976 and 1990, Koreans formed the third largest group of immigrants to America, after the Mexican and Filipino communities.

As of the 2010 **census**, there were approximately 1.7 million people of Korean descent residing in the United States. In 2017, almost half of the Korean American population lived in three states: California, New York, and New Jersey. In 2005, the US Senate and

House of Representatives passed a resolution recognizing January 13 as Korean American Day. This day **commemorates** and celebrates the contributions and impact that the Korean American community has made and continues to make in America.

CHAPTER THREE
CHAMPION IN THE MAKING

While studying to be a doctor, Sammy continued to enter diving competitions. He hoped to qualify for the next Olympic Games in Helsinki, Finland, but because of World War II, the 1940 Olympics were canceled. Sammy was crushed. He thought his dream of becoming an Olympic champion had ended.

In 1943 Sammy's father suffered a heart attack and died. Sammy was devastated.

Then he remembered his father's shoebox—the one filled with money for Sammy's future. He could not let his father's dream die.

Sammy took a break from diving and worked hard to get accepted into a special United States Army medical training program. He discovered he did have a passion for medicine and became a doctor in 1946.

Sammy started working at different hospitals in California, but he still missed diving. So he found a pool near each hospital and practiced diving after his shifts ended. Still dreaming of the Olympics, Sammy entered the national diving championship in 1946. Even though he did not have much time to train for the event, Sammy won the high-platform dive with the highest score ever.

Despite his achievements, Sammy continued to face discrimination. Once, after performing at a diving exhibition with his friends, Sammy was forbidden from entering a restaurant to have dinner with them. And Sammy was still **restricted** from using some pools except on assigned days.

Instead of getting angry over such unfair treatment, Sammy decided to prove his worth at the upcoming 1948 Olympic Games in London. He received special permission from the army to take time off for his training.

Asians in California: Opportunity & Discrimination

The first significant group of Asian immigrants to the United States arrived between 1849 and 1852, when around 23,000 Chinese men journeyed to California seeking wealth and **prosperity** during the **California Gold Rush.** A lucky few found gold; however, the majority needed to find work to survive. By 1860, over 70 percent of Chinese men in California worked in mines, while others set up businesses like restaurants and laundry services near mining areas. Between 1862 and 1869, approximately 12,000 Chinese men built the **Transcontinental Railroad.** These men made up 90 percent of the railroad workforce.

Working on the railroad was a dangerous job, especially in harsh weather conditions. The Chinese men worked longer hours and for less pay than their white coworkers. When they went on strike demanding equal pay, reasonable work hours, and better living conditions, the director of Central Pacific (the company responsible for building the railroad) cut off the Chinese workers' food supply. Chinese laborers were forced to continue working at their original wage and conditions until the railroad was completed. More than 1,200 Chinese men lost their lives building the railroad.

After the railroad was completed, thousands of Chinese laborers decided to settle in San Francisco, where they made up half of the workforce in the city's shoe, textile, and cigar factories. Others took jobs in agriculture and construction—about 95 percent of the Chinese population in Sacramento and San Joaquin worked on farms. Yet no matter the task, Chinese workers were paid less than white workers performing the same job. By the 1900s, Chinese immigrants began to spread out across the United States and support themselves by opening small businesses, restaurants, laundromats, and stores.

American businesses continued to recruit workers from other Asian countries to fill their labor needs. By the 1930s, 140,000 Japanese, 56,000 Filipinos, and several thousand Korean and Asian Indian immigrants were

Chinese immigrant men working on the Transcontinental Railroad, 1869.

living in America. Most of them resided in California. Asian immigrants were often seen as competition for jobs and a threat to the economy by white Americans.

Asians residing in America faced racism and discrimination in other areas of their lives besides the workplace. They were often refused service in theaters, restaurants, beauty salons, clothing stores, and hotels. If they were allowed to enter, they had to sit in separate areas from whites or wait to be served after white customers. Housing segregation also took place. Asian immigrants were often told "No Orientals

Allowed" when moving to a mostly white neighborhood. This led to the formation of Chinatowns, Little Manilas, and Little Tokyos—communities established by Asian immigrants, which provided them with a safe place to gather and create their own boardinghouses, social halls, churches, and restaurants.

After Japan bombed Pearl Harbor in Honolulu, Hawaii, in December 1941 and America entered World War II, Japanese Americans were seen as the enemy by many white Americans. Around 20,000 first-, second-, and third-generation Japanese people living on the West Coast lost their homes and businesses and were forced to move into camps and live in prisonlike conditions for four years by the US government. Also, Japan occupied Korea at this time, which made the US government **suspicious** of Koreans, thinking they might be allied with Japan. Many white Americans started to see Koreans as the enemy. Although Korean Americans did not have to move into the camps, the US government froze their assets and placed the same restrictions on them as they did Japanese Americans. During and after the war, Korean American businesses became the target of hate crimes and **vandalism.** Meanwhile, Chinese, Filipino, and South Asians were considered to be "good Asians" by white Americans, since their homeland countries were allied with the United States during the war.

During this time, Asians in America became proactive in participating in the war efforts. Organizations like the Chinese War Relief Association raised funds from over 300 Chinese communities across North and South America. Others volunteered for service,

Two storefronts in San Francisco, California, 1942. The store on the left has a sign in the window to let shoppers know it's owned by someone of Chinese descent. The store on the right is operated by a person of Japanese descent who is running an "evacuation sale".

bought war bonds, and worked in shipyards. After the First Lady of the Republic of China, Madame Chiang Kai-shek, met with President Roosevelt and spoke to Congress, the US Women's Army Corps recruited a Chinese American unit to serve with the US Army Air Forces. Japanese American women also served as military translators.

It was not until the late 1940s and 1950s that Asians in the US were allowed to become citizens, vote, and marry **interracially.** The 1960s marked the beginning of Asian American activists uniting together to challenge "**passive**" stereotypes and **advocate** for equal pay in the workforce, fair housing practices, and **ethnic studies** classes in universities. In 1968, Yuji Ichioka, who taught the first Asian American studies class at UCLA, created the term "Asian American" to unite the different ethnic Asian students and reject the term "Oriental," which had become a historically **discriminatory** term. In 2010, approximately 5.6 million Asian Americans resided in California and made up about 15 percent of the state's population.

CHAPTER FOUR
OLYMPIC MOMENT

At the age of twenty-eight, Sammy qualified to be a member of the US Olympic diving team. The diving competition was held at the Empire Pool in Wembley Stadium in London. Sammy was in awe as he entered the stadium. Here he was, the son of Korean immigrants, representing the United States at the Olympics. He knew his family would be proud.

Sammy's first event was the three-meter springboard dive. He was nervous, and the excitement was almost unbearable. At previous competitions,

Sammy would usually put lamb's wool in his ears to block out the noise of the crowd so he could concentrate. But Sammy was finally at the Olympics. He didn't want to miss a thing. He took out his earplugs so he could hear everything.

Sammy stood on the diving board. He was sure everyone could hear his heart beating. Then he focused himself, jumped high, and made one of his best dives ever. It won him the bronze medal.

Sammy was happy but not satisfied. He wanted to win a gold medal. He knew his strength lay in the upcoming ten-meter platform event. Here was his chance to show he was the greatest diver in the world.

Right before the event, Sammy heard a rumor that there might be some **prejudice** against him because he wasn't white. This only added to his determination to win.

Sammy remained calm. "I'm going for the gold," he told his teammates before climbing up the ladder. He no longer wanted to win just for

himself. He wanted to win to prove that no one should be judged by the color of his or her skin.

For his final dive in the ten-meter platform event, Sammy decided to perform the forward three and a half somersault. This was a very dangerous move. The slightest **miscalculation** in timing could lead to a serious, even fatal, injury.

Sammy faced a crowd of thousands. His mouth was dry. He heard the sound of water lapping against the sides of the pool, the murmuring of the people, the beating of his heart.

Never before had Sammy felt such intense pressure. He had trained sixteen years for this—a moment that would last barely sixteen seconds from the time he dived to when the scores would be revealed.

Sammy closed his eyes, and in his mind he was twelve years old again. It was Wednesday at the pool. He and Hart were practicing somersaults. Somehow, this image calmed Sammy's nerves. He opened his eyes, took a deep breath, and leaped

off the platform.

Sammy flew through the air. He did one . . . then two . . . then three . . . and a half somersaults!

The crowd gasped.

As Sammy broke the surface, drops of water trickled over his eyes. He shook his head and blinked. Then he saw the scores.

7.0   9.0   9.5   9.5
9.5   9.5

And then . . . 10.0. *Ten!* He had a perfect score!

Sammy Lee became the first Korean American to win a gold medal.

Diving at the Olympics

Diving first became a popular sport in Germany during the eighteenth century. Gymnasts would stand at the edge of a pool and do acrobatic moves as they tumbled into the water. In the late nineteenth century, Swedish divers performed popular diving displays, and Swedes started the Amateur Diving Association in 1901.

The earliest recorded diving competition took place in 1871 off the London Bridge. Diving first became an Olympic sport at the 1904 Games in St. Louis, Missouri, where it was called Fancy Diving. Separate springboard and platform events were introduced at the 1908 Olympics in London. It was not until the 1912 Stockholm Olympics that women were able to dive as well.

Unlike swimming, where the person with the fastest time wins, divers are awarded gold, silver, and bronze medals based on their overall diving scores. A panel of seven judges gives scores between 0 and 10, in half-point **increments.** A score of 0 is a failure while a score of 10 is perfect. Judges look for the following when deciding what score to give:

- A smooth, yet strong *approach*. The approach is the steps the diver takes toward the edge of the board before the hurdle and takeoff. The *hurdle* is the last steps the diver takes in their approach. It allows the diver to position themselves properly for the dive while maintaining or building momentum for their takeoff.

- A controlled and balanced *takeoff*. The takeoff is the diver's leap from the board before performing the dive.

- A high *elevation*. The elevation is the height the diver achieves upon takeoff, which can affect the accuracy and gracefulness of the diver's execution.

- The *execution,* which is how well the specific dive is performed. Judges look for **precision**, proper form, and grace.

- The dive *entry*. The diver should enter the water with the smallest splash possible. It should sound like a "rip," or the tearing of paper.

After each of the seven judges awards a score to the diver, the two highest and lowest scores are taken out. The remaining scores are added together and then multiplied by a **predetermined** number based on the difficulty of the dive, which can range from 1.2 to 4.1 in one-tenth increments.

In 2000, **synchronized** diving, which consists of two divers performing the same dive at the exact same time, was introduced in the Sydney Olympic Games.

Jingjing Guo and Minxia Wu of the People's Republic of China compete in the three-meter synchronized diving event at the World Aquatics Championships in Rome, Italy, 2009.

The judging and scoring of a synchronized dive is similar to a solo dive, except there are eleven judges and five of the judges score the synchronization of the two divers.

CHAPTER FIVE
GOLDEN GLORY

Sammy stood on the podium as his United States flag was raised high. *I did it*, he thought, beaming with pride. He had won the gold medal, not only for himself, but for his father, Coach Ryan, and Hart Crum. He had also won the gold for his country. Someday, he hoped, all swimming pools would be open every day of the week for all Americans.

The crowd roared. Voices filled the **cavernous** stadium, but all Sammy could hear were his father's words: "In America, you can achieve anything if you set your heart to it."

After the 1948 Olympics, Sammy served as a doctor in the

Korean War. Then, in the 1952 Olympic Games in Helsinki, Finland, Sammy became the first man ever to defend an Olympic platform-diving title. He was also the first male diver to win gold medals for diving in two successive Olympics.

In 1953, Sammy was the first Asian American awarded the James E. Sullivan Award. This award is given annually by the Amateur Athletic Union to the top amateur athlete in the United States. It is considered the most

prestigious sports award in the country. Sammy coached diver Bob Webster to Olympic gold medals in 1960 and 1964, and Greg Louganis to a silver medal at the 1976 Olympic Games.

Sammy married Rosalind M. K. Wong in 1950. He lived in California and had two children and three grandchildren. He remained an active athlete throughout his life—in his nineties, he still swam laps at his local pool every day. Dr. Sammy Lee passed away on December 2, 2016, in California, leaving behind an inspirational legacy for all athletes.

Greg Louganis

Greg Louganis was born in California in 1960 and began excelling in gymnastics and acrobatics at the age of three. By nine years old, he was a seasoned performer and competitor in local talent competitions. Around the same time, his family had a swimming pool built in their backyard. Greg practiced gymnastic stunts into the pool but often landed on his back. Seeing his enthusiasm for diving, and wanting to protect him from getting hurt, his mom signed him up for diving lessons.

By age 11, Greg placed second in the one-meter springboard event at the National Junior Olympics. Dr. Sammy Lee saw Greg dive and was impressed. He believed Greg had the potential to make the 1976 Olympic team and agreed to coach him twice a week.

At 16, Greg qualified for the 1976 Olympic diving team and won a silver medal in the ten-meter platform event. Two years later, Greg began training with Ron O'Brien, who coached him for the remainder of his Olympic career.

The United States **boycotted** the 1980 Olympic Games in Moscow, so Greg could not participate. Still, he continued training, and he competed against the 1980 Olympic gold medalist diver in the World Championship two years later. After performing an inward one and a half pike dive off the ten-meter platform, Greg became the first diver in a major international meet to get perfect 10s from all seven judges! Greg won the title in both platform and springboard events. Greg's ability to perform difficult dives with precise and graceful execution allowed him to dominate the sport of diving in the years to come.

Greg went on to win gold medals in both the springboard- and platform-diving events at the 1984 Olympic Games in Los Angeles. During the 1988 preliminary rounds in Seoul, he unexpectedly hit his head on the springboard while completing a dive. He needed four stitches and struggled with the embarrassment and pain of his injury. Yet he did not give up. Greg completed his last two dives and made the final round. He won the gold medal again in the springboard event

Diver Greg Louganis competing in the 10-meter platform event during the US Diving Indoor Championships in Indianapolis, IN, April 20, 1986.

and came from behind to win gold in the platform event. Greg became the first male diver in history to win both events in back-to-back Olympic Games.

Upon winning his fourth and fifth Olympic gold medals in the 1988 Games, Greg retired from diving at the age of 28. He spent the next several years pursuing acting and making public appearances. In 1994, Greg came out as gay, and the next year, he announced he was HIV positive. Soon after, Greg's autobiography *Breaking the Surface* was released, detailing his struggle living with secrets before and after his Olympic career. He compares telling the truth about his life to training and preparing for the Olympics—one of the biggest challenges he ever faced, but also the most rewarding. He continues to support and serve on the board for amfAR, The Foundation for AIDS Research, and is an active member of the Human Rights Campaign, which advocates for basic equal rights of the LGBTQ community.

TIMELINE

1920   August 1: Sammy Lee is born in Fresno, CA

1938   Competes in a diving competition where he meets his coach Jim Ryan

1939   Graduates from Benjamin Franklin High School

1943   Graduates from Occidental College

1946   Enters the national diving championship and takes first place in the high-platform dive

1947   Graduates from the University of Southern California medical school and becomes an ear, nose, and throat specialist. Serves as an army major and medical officer in the Korean War

1948   Competes in the Olympic Games in London and wins a bronze medal in the three-meter springboard event and a gold medal in the ten-meter platform. Just two days earlier, Filipino American diver Victoria Manalo Draves won gold medals at the same Olympic Games, making her the first Asian American to win an Olympic medal, and Dr. Lee the first Asian American man to accomplish this.

1950   Marries Rosalind M. K. Wong

1952 Competes in the Olympic Games in Helsinki, Finland, and wins gold, making him the first male diver to medal in two successive Olympics

1953 Awarded the James E. Sullivan Award by the Amateur Athletic Union.

1955 Opens medical practice in Orange County, CA

1960 Coaches the US diving team at the Olympic Games in Rome, Italy

1968 Elected to the International Swimming Hall of Fame

1990 Retires from medical practice after 35 years of service
Elected to the United States Olympic Hall of Fame

2010 The corner of Olympic Blvd. and Normandie Ave. in Los Angeles, CA, is named Sammy Lee Square

2016 December 2: Dies in Newport Beach, California

GLOSSARY

acrobatic (AAH-kro-BAH-tik) *adjective* having the qualities of an acrobat, like gymnastic skills, flexibility, and strength

advocate (AD-voh-kate) *verb* to publicly support and peacefully fight for a cause or group of people

arch (aarch) *verb* to bend into a curved shape

bachelor (BAA-chuh-lur) *noun* an unmarried man

berate (bur-AY-ting) *verb* to scold in an angry way

boycott (BOI-kot): *verb* to avoid doing business with a company or organization to protest its actions; *noun* the act of boycotting a place

California Gold Rush (kal-ee-FOR-nee-ah gold rush) *proper noun* a historical event that lasted from 1848–1855. After gold was found in Coloma, California, 300,000 people from across the US and around the world came to the area in the hopes of finding gold and becoming wealthy

cavernous (KA-ver-nis) *adjective* a large, cave-like space

census (SEN-suhs) *noun* a count of all the people in a particular country. In the United States, a census is held every ten years

Chinese Exclusion Act (CHI-nees eks-KLOO-shun akt) *proper noun* a federal law signed in 1882 that prohibited Chinese workers from immigrating to the US. It was the first major act of legislation to restrict immigration to the US

commemorate (kuh-MEM-ur-ate) *verb* to do something to remember an important person or historical event

discrimination (diss-krim-uh-NAY-shun) *noun* the act of treating some people better than others, usually for a prejudiced or unfair reason

discriminatory (diss-KRIM-in-nuh-toh-ree) *adjective* engaging in discrimination

emigration (eh-mih-GRAY-shun) *noun* the act of leaving a country or region to live somewhere else; immigration is the act of coming to a country or region to live

envy (EN-vee) *noun* the feeling of wanting something that belongs to someone else

ethnic studies (ETH-nik STUH-deez) *noun* an academic subject area that focuses on race, ethnicity, and the experiences of people of color in and outside of the United States

execute (EK-sih-kuwt) *verb* to do or perform

Immigration Act of 1924 (eh-mih-GRAY-shun akt) *proper noun* a federal law signed in 1924 that used a quota system to limit the number of immigrants entering the US

Immigration and Nationality Act of 1952 (eh-mih-GRAY-shun and NASH-un-al-it-ee akt) *proper noun* federal legislation signed in 1952 that ended the Oriental Exclusion Act, allowing Asian immigrants to become US citizens, but still enforced a quota system that continued to limit the number of immigrants from Asian countries

Immigration and Nationality Act of 1965 (eh-mih-GRAY-shun and NASH-un-al-it-ee akt) *proper noun* federal legislation signed in 1965 that made it illegal to prohibit a person from immigrating to the US on the basis of their race, ancestry, or nation of origin

increment (IN-kruh-ment) *noun* the measure of how much smaller or larger something becomes

instability (in-stuh-BIL-uh-tee) *noun* a state in which conditions are not likely to stay the same

interracially (in-tur-RAY-shuh-lee) *adverb* involving different races of people

Korean War (ko-REE-in WOR) *proper noun* a conflict between North Korea and South Korea that took place from 1950–1953

legislation (leh-jus-LAY-shun) *noun* bills considered and laws made by a government

minimum wage (MI-nuh-mum WAYJ) *noun* the lowest wage that can be paid to an hourly employee, as set by local, state, or federal law

miscalculation (mis-kal-kew-LAY-shun) *noun* a mistake in figuring out the size or amount of something

lousiest (LAU-zee-ist) *adjective* the worst or poorest

passive (PAA-siv) *adjective* allowing things to happen without trying to change the situation

precision (pruh-SI-zhun): *noun* the quality of being exact

predetermined (pre-duh-TUR-mihnd) *adjective* decided ahead of time

prejudice (PREH-juh-dis) *noun* a feeling of dislike for a person or group because of their race, religion, age, or sex

prosperity (praw-SPEHR-uh-tee) *noun* success in terms of having a lot of money and a comfortable life

recruiters (ree-KROO-turz) *noun* people whose job it is to get others to join a company, business, or service

reputation (reh-puh-TAY-shun) *noun* overall opinions that people have about someone or something

restricted (ree-STRIK-tid) *adjective* not allowed

somersault (SUM-mur-salt) *verb* a movement that involves turning or flipping forward or backward

suspicious (sus-PIH-shus) *adjective* having a feeling that someone or something cannot be trusted

synchronize (SYN-kro-nize) *verb* to make two or more things happen at the same time or speed

Transcontinental Railroad (trans-KON-tuh-nen-tul RAIL-rowd) *proper noun* a railroad system built between 1862 and 1869 that connected the East and West Coasts of the United States

vandalism (VAN-duh-lih-zum) *noun* the act of destroying or damaging property on purpose

War Bride Act (WOR BRYDE AKT) *proper noun* a federal law signed in 1946 that allowed spouses, natural children, and adopted children of members of the US Armed Forces to enter the United States

World War II (WURLD WOR TOO) *proper noun* a conflict involving more than thirty countries from 1939 to 1945, fought mainly in Europe, North Africa, Asia, and the South Pacific

TEXT SOURCES

Ku, Beulah. "Sammy Lee—Olympic Pioneer." *Asian Week*, vol. 13, no. 47 (July 17, 1992): 11.

Lee, Sammy. "An Olympians Oral History: Sammy Lee." Interview by Dr. Margaret Costa. Amateur Athletics Foundation of Los Angeles (December, 1999). https://digital.la84.org/digital/collection/p17103coll11/id/216/.

McFadden, Robert, D. "Sammy Lee, First Asian-American Man to Earn Olympic Gold, Dies at 96." The *New York Times*. Last updated December 4, 2016. https://www.nytimes.com/2016/12/03/sports/sammy-lee-dies-asian-american-olympic-gold.html

USC Athletics "Two-Time Olympic Gold Medal Diver Dr. Sammy Lee, USC's Oldest Surviving Olympian, Dies." Last modified December 3, 2016. https://usctrojans.com/news/2016/12/3/two_time_olympic_gold_medal_diver_dr_sammy_lee_usc_s_oldest_surviving_olympian_dies.aspx

Wampler, Molly Frick. *Not Without Honor: The Story of Sammy Lee*. Santa Barbara: The Fithian Press, 1987.

SIDEBAR SOURCES

DIVING INTO DIVING

British Swimming. "History of Diving." Accessed April 12, 2019. https://www.britishswimming.org/browse-sport/diving/learn-more-about-diving/history-diving/.

"Diving, springboard and platform." *The Columbia Encyclopedia*, 6th ed. New York: Columbia University Press, 2000. Accessed April 12, 2019. https://www.encyclopedia.com/sports-and-everyday-life/sports/sports/springboard-and-platform-diving.

"Diving." *Encyclopaedia Britannica*, 8th ed. Chicago: Encyclopaedia Britannica, 2009. Accessed April 12, 2019. https://www.britannica.com/sports/diving.

Lanser, Amanda. *The Science Behind Swimming, Diving, and Other Water Sports.* Science of the Summer Olympics. North Mankato, MN: Capstone Books, 2016.

Olympic Studies Center. "Aquatics: History of diving at the Olympic Games." Last modified March 2015. Accessed April 12, 2019. https://www.olympic.org/diving-equipment-and-history.

The Public Domain Review. "Olympic Diving Diagrams (1912)." Accessed April 12, 2019. https://publicdomainreview.org/collections/olympic-diving-diagrams-1912/.

Swim England Diving. "About platform and springboard diving." Last modified March 16, 2016. Accessed April 12, 2019. https://www.swimming.org/diving/about-platform-and-springboard-diving/.

HOW KOREANS CAME TO THE UNITED STATES

Boston Korean Diaspora Project. "History of Korean Immigration to America, from 1903 to Present." Accessed April 8, 2019. http://sites.bu.edu/koreandiaspora/issues/history-of-korean-immigration-to-america-from-1903- to-present/.

Boundless staff writers. "Immigration in the 1960s." *Boundless* (blog). Last modified July 3, 2017. Accessed April 14, 2019. https://www.boundless.com/blog/60s-immigration/.

Center for Immigration Studies. "The Legacy of the 1965 Immigration Act." Accessed April 8, 2019. https://cis.org/Report/Legacy-1965-Immigration-Act.

Kim, Ilpyong J. *Korean-Americans: Past, Present, and Future.* Elizabeth, N. J.: Hollym International Corporation, 2004.

Korea Economic Institute of America. "History of Korean American Day." Accessed April 14, 2019. http://keia.org/page/history-korean-american-day.

Lee, Cristina. "Minding Their Own Businesses: Entrepreneurs: Up to 40% of the Southland's Korean immigrants own their own companies. They run 70% of Orange County's dry cleaners and 27% of its neighborhood grocery stores." *Los Angeles Times*, September 10, 1991. Accessed April 8, 2019. https://www.latimes.com/archives/la-xpm-1991-09-10-fi-2531-story.html.

Nakamura, Kelli Y. "Picture brides." *Densho Encyclopedia*. Accessed April 14, 2019. http://encyclopedia.densho.org/Picture_brides/.

O'Connor, Allison and Jeanne Batalova. "Korean Immigrants in the United States." Migration Policy Institute. Last Modified April 10, 2019. Accessed April 14, 2019. https://www.migrationpolicy.org/article/korean-immigrants-united-states.

United States Census Bureau. *The Asian Population: 2010*. Washington, DC: United States Department of Commerce, Economics and Statistics Administration, 2002. https://www.census.gov/prod/cen2010/briefs/c2010br-11.pdf.

ASIANS IN CALIFORNIA: OPPORTUNITY AND DISCRIMINATION

Ancheta, Angelo N. *Race, Rights, and the Asian American Experience*. New Brunswick, N. J.: Rutgers University Press, 2006.

"Asian Americans, Impact of the Great Depression On." *Encyclopedia of the the Great Depression*. New York: Macmillan Library Reference, 2003. Accessed April 14, 2019. https://www.encyclopedia.com/economics/ encyclopedias-almanacs-transcripts-and-maps/ asian-americans-impact-great-depression.

Le, Cuong N. "The First Asian Americans." *Asian Nation* (blog). Accessed April 14, 2019. http://www. asian-nation.org/first.shtml#sthash.MZRqTffW. dpbs.

Lee, Erika. *The Making of Asian America: A History*. New York: Simon & Schuster, 2015.

Library of Congress. The Transcontinental Railroad. Accessed July 18, 2019. https://www.loc.gov/ collections/railroad-maps-1828-to-1900/articles- and-essays/history-of-railroads-and-maps/the- transcontinental-railroad/.

Japanese American Citizens' League. *The Journey from Gold Mountain: The Asian American Experience*. San Francisco: Japanese American Citizen's League, 2006.

PBS. "Chinese Immigrants and the Gold Rush."
Accessed April 14, 2019. https://www.pbs.
org/wgbh/americanexperience/features/
goldrush-chinese-immigrants/.

Pimentel, Joseph. "Study reveals Asians face
housing discrimination." *Asian Journal*. Last
modified June 19, 2013. Accessed April 20,
2019. https://www.asianjournal.com/usa/
study-reveals-asians-face-housing-discrimination.

Wallace, Nina. "Yellow Power: The Origins of Asian
America." *Densho* (blog). Accessed June 2, 2019.
https://densho.org/asian-american-movement.

DIVING AT THE OLYMPICS

The Conversation. "Not making a splash: The anatomy of
a perfect Olympic Dive." Last modified July 30, 2012.
Accessed April 12, 2019. https://theconversation.
com/not-making-a-splash-the-anatomy-of-a-
perfect-olympic-dive-8082.

From the Lab Bench. "Olympic Diving Physics."
Last modified August 7, 2012. Accessed April
12, 2019. http://www.fromthelabbench.
com/from-the-lab-bench-science-blog/
olympic-diving-physics.

Grannan, Cydney. "How Is Diving Scored?" *Encyclopaedia Britannica*, 8th ed. Chicago: Encyclopedia Britannica, 2009. Accessed April 12, 2019. https://www.britannica.com/story/how-is-diving-scored.

USA Diving. "Diving 101: Judging and Scoring." Accessed April 12, 2019. https://www.teamusa.org/USA-Diving/About-Us/Diving-101/Judging-and-Scoring.

GREG LOUGANIS

Furjanic, Cheryl, dir. *Back on Board: Greg Louganis*. Aired August 4, 2014, on HBO. https://www.amazon.com/Back-Board-Greg-Louganis/dp/B01JJYL8YY/ref=sr_1_3?crid=36HFGXEQCNLXW&keywords=breaking+the+surface+the+greg+louganis+story&qid=1556806191&s=instant-video&sprefix=breaking+the+surface%2Cinstant video%2C494&sr=1-3-catcorr.

Louganis, Greg, and Eric Marcus. *Breaking the Surface*. Chicago: Sourcebooks, 2014.

Worldwide Management. "Greg Louganis, 4x Gold Medal Olympic Champion." *Dive In*. Accessed April 20, 2019. https://greglouganis.com/.

RECOMMENDED FURTHER READING

Fiction books are marked with an asterisk (*).

DIVING AND YOUNG ATHLETES

Billingsley, Hobie. *Competitive Diving: The Complete Guide for Coaches, Divers, Judges*. California: Trius Publishing, 2018.

* Binns, Barbara. *Courage*. New York: HarperCollins, 2019.

Ignotofsky, Rachel. *Women in Sports: 50 Fearless Athletes Who Played to Win*. Women in Science. New York: Penguin Random House, 2017.

Lanser, Amanda. *The Science Behind Swimming, Diving, and Other Water Sports*. Science of the Summer Olympics. North Mankato, MN: Capstone Books, 2016.

Stabler, David. *Kid Athletes: True Tales of Childhood from Sports Legends*. Kid Legends. Philadelphia: Quirk Books, 2015.

ASIAN IMMIGRANTS IN CALIFORNIA

Freedman, Russell. *Angel Island: Gateway to Gold Mountain*. Boston: Houghton Mifflin Harcourt, 2016.

* Honeyman, Kay. *The Fire Horse Girl*. New York: Arthur A. Levine Books, 2013.

* Na, An. *A Step from Heaven*. New York: Atheneum Books for Young Readers, 2016.

* Yang, Kelly. *Front Desk*. New York: Arthur A. Levine Books, 2018.

Yoo, Paula. *The Story of Movie Star Anna May Wong*. New York: Lee & Low Books, 2019.

THE OLYMPICS AND OLYMPIC ATHLETES

Bruchac, Joseph. *Jim Thorpe: Original All-American*. New York: Dial Books, 2006.

———. *The Story of All-Star Athlete Jim Thorpe*. New York: Lee & Low Books, 2019.

Crowe, Ellie. *The Story of Olympic Swimmer Duke Kahanamoku*. New York: Lee & Low Books, 2019.

Herman, Gail. *What Are the Summer Olympics?* What Was?. New York: Penguin Random House, 2016.

Time-Life. *The Olympics: Moments That Made History*. Tampa, FL: Time Inc. Books, 2016.

ABOUT THE AUTHOR

PAULA YOO is an author and screenwriter whose children's books for Lee & Low include *Sixteen Years in Sixteen Seconds*, *Shining Star*, and several titles in the Confetti Kids series. Her titles have been recognized by the International Literacy Association, the Texas Bluebonnet Award Master List, and Lee & Low's New Voices Award. She and her husband live in Los Angeles, California, where she works in television. You can visit her online at paulayoo.com.

ABOUT THE ILLUSTRATOR

DOM LEE was born in Seoul, South Korea, and received his MFA from the School of Visual Arts in New York City. With his unique style of art combining techniques of painting and scratching details in encaustic wax, Lee has illustrated many award-winning picture books for Lee & Low Books. He and his wife live in Hollis, New York. To find out more about Dom Lee, visit domandk.com